THiS BOOK BELONGS TO

AND MANY MORE
iLLUSTRATIONS...................

IT'S TIME
to
Believe
IN YOU

Stay Humble

EVERY
THING
STARTS WITH A
DREAM

LIFE
LAUGH
LOVE

Love
FOR ALL
Hatred
FOR
NONE

ENERGIZE
your
LIFE

Stay
Positive
&
Good Thin
Will
Happen

BE
Brave
WITH YOUR
Life

the best is yet to come

love
is
love

IT ALWAYS
Seems
IMPOSSIBLE
UNTIL
ITS
done

LIFE IS
A JOURNEY
ENJOY
THE
RIDE

I ACCEPT MYSELF AS I AM

BE
YOUR
OWN
HERO

Take a
small
step
everyday

THERE'S A WAY
TO DO IT
better
FIND IT

EVERY
EXPERT
WAS ONCE A
Beginner

YOU ARE
STRONGER
than you
THINK

Think
HAPPY
thoughts

Smile
&
Shine

NEVER STOP
Smiling

Beautiful minds inspire others

See the
GOOD
IN EVERY
Situation

ALWAY
Believe
IN
YOURSELF

MISTAKES
ARE
PROOF
THAT YOU ARE
TRYING

More
Self
Love

FORGET THE
MISTAKE
REMEMBER
THE
LESSON

BE
Strong
AND
Courageous

I ♥ love
your
self

You
DESERVE
TO BE
Happy

THINK
OUTSIDE
THE
BOX

you're
unique

Good
THINGS
come
to those
WHO
Wait

Don't wait
for a
OPORTUNIT
Create it

Stop Talking Start Doing

Today
is
gonna
to be
a
Great
Day

Create
Each Day
Anew

DREAM IT
WISH IT
and
DO IT

Make Today better

Pray More
WORRY LESS

HOPE YOU HAVE PASSED A WONDERFULL TIME PLEASE LEAVE A REVIEW. YOUR REVIEW WOULD ENCOURAGE US TO MAKE MORE CREATIVE CONTENTS